Christmas in America

Preceding page: Amid the hustle and bustle of Christmas in Miami, Florida, there's always time for a whispered conversation with Santa. *This page:* Bringing home the Christmas tree, Vermont style—on skis!

Christmas in America

Nancy S. Grant

CRESCENT BOOKS

NEW YORK

The only thing these 13 New Yorkers appear to have
in common are twinkling eyes and merry grins. . .

. . . but oh, what a transformation!

*This 1991 edition published by CRESCENT BOOKS
distributed by Outlet Book Company, Inc.,
a Random House Company,
225 Park Avenue South, New York, New York 10003*

ISBN 0-517-06573-8

87654321

Printed and bound in Hong Kong

*For rights information about the photographs in
this book please contact:*

*The Image Bank
111 Fifth Avenue, New York, New York 10003*

Producer: *Solomon M. Skolnick*
Writer: *Nancy S. Grant*
Designer: *Ann-Louise Lipman*
Editor: *Sara Colacurto*
Production: *Valerie Zars*
Photo Researcher: *Edward Douglas*
Assistant Photo Researcher: *Robert V. Hale*
Editorial Assistant: *Carol Raguso*

Preceding page: **A glittering mosaic
of ornaments, garlands, and electric
lights turns a Chicago tree into a
holiday delight.**

A ah, Christmas is in the air—from the wafts of spicy, sweetly tantalizing aromas drifting out of kitchens from Albany to Anaheim, to the merry jingling of sleigh bells near Minneapolis, to the faint rustle of evergreen needles as another brightly wrapped package takes its place under a twinkling tree in Montgomery. Listen, and you will hear children in Schenectady, St. Louis, and Sacramento begging, as bedtime draws near, "Just one more Christmas story, please, please!"

But which Christmas story to tell? As Americans make ready to celebrate with family and friends, there are two obvious choices—Luke's wondrous Gospel of the Nativity, or Clement C. Moore's enchanting poem "A Visit from Saint Nicholas." Each, in its own way, calls to mind a host of holiday traditions and memories, of hopes and dreams renewed each December.

Holy day and holiday, sacred and sumptuous, the Light of the World and worldly delights—the two sides of Christmas in America beckon to us, inviting us to lay aside our workaday worries and join in the celebration. And Americans, being an ingenious lot, continue to think up new variations on old themes, mingling religious convictions and folk customs into something distinctly American.

Christmas Comes to America

By the third week of December, beleaguered parents mumble, "Is it choir practice tonight and the school pageant tomorrow, or the other way around?" At the local shopping mall you'll hear a frazzled shopper grumble, "Does this gizmo come *with* batteries, or am I going to have to stand in line *again*?" The days may be getting shorter, but the list of things to do keeps getting

longer—until someone suddenly exclaims, "Surely Christmas was simpler for our forefathers!"

Indeed, the first English colonists to celebrate Christmas in America in 1607 coped with an altogether different sort of mid-winter confusion. Just seven months earlier, 100 bold settlers had splashed hopefully ashore to what is now Virginia—but as the weak December sun slanted through the trees and underbrush surrounding their tiny enclave, more than half had already perished. Disease, battles with the local native inhabitants, even outright starvation had each taken their toll; for those weary men and women remaining, that first Christmas in America wasn't just simple—it was downright bare.

After bone-wearying, perilous days struggling for survival, they may have passed the long winter evenings recounting tales of Christmas back home in England. There, Yuletide meant visiting with family and friends, and feasting, frolicking, singing, and dancing near huge bonfires—but in their new home such recollections brought tears to eyes already stinging from cold winter winds. Heartsick, homesick, uncertain of their future, they nevertheless gathered together on December 25 in the rough wooden chapel of their fort to reaffirm their faith in God. They marked the anniversary of Jesus' birth with Bible readings and heartfelt prayers—especially for their leader, Captain John Smith, whereabouts unknown, seeking corn and other foodstuffs from any natives not intent on destroying him and his people.

But by the next year, John Smith, his company of settlers—and Christmas—had survived the trials of life in a new land. Though "extreame winde, rayne, frost and snow caused us to keepe Christmas among the salvages [sic]," these hardy Virginians bragged, "we were never more merry, nor fed on more plenty of good Oysters,

Fish, Flesh, Wilde fowl and good bread, nor never had better fires in England."

As more and more English settlers took up land in tidewater Virginia and farther south, good old-fashioned English bonfires, roaring and crackling merrily, were soon setting the December skies aglow above the American wilderness. Caroling, capering, feasting, and drinking was the order of the day—and night—from the first fortified communities to far-flung plantations. The air reverberated with one of the first New World additions to Christmas merry-making: the din of horns and drums, firecrackers and gunpowder, all boisterously announcing a welcome break from work routines.

That was definitely not the case farther north. When the Puritan Pilgrims landed in Massachusetts in 1620, they were heartily sick of the excessive celebrations that had grown up around religious occasions in the Old World. They spent *their* first Christmas Day hammering and sawing timber to build houses, steadfastly refusing to treat that day as different from any other. Church leaders, who were also the community's political leaders, made it a crime to do so much as wish someone a "Merry Christmas" or bake plum puddings and mince pies. Yet as the settlement prospered, in private homes, many a good housewife searched her larder for likely American substitutes for the traditional ingredients, chose a pan of a different shape, and pleased her family in secret.

Meanwhile, French and Spanish colonists were establishing toeholds elsewhere on the vast continent, bringing along their own Christmas traditions of hunting and sporting contests, as well as plays and pageants reenacting the events of the Nativity. French children left their shoes by the *crèche*, or Nativity scene, in hopes that during the night the Baby Jesus himself would fill them with gifts. Dutch colonists in 1624 brought along the legend of "Sinterklass," a red-robed bishop on horseback who left his treats for good little

children on the hearth. Scandinavians, who first arrived in 1628, brought along stories of gift-giving elves, as well as the custom of hanging a fir or pine bough wreath on their front doors.

In the 1700's, as the Colonial era got into full swing, decorating with greenery, gathering with family and friends for cheery toasts and ample meals, home-made (there wasn't any other kind!) candies and treats for the children, trouping off to church services, singing in the streets and around glowing hearths—in the New World these simple pleasures were combined in varying proportions and details according to each community's Old World origins.

Mid-winter was the logical time for such merry-making, for the colonists' year revolved around agriculture and the dictates of the weather. The heavy labor of spring planting was followed relentlessly by the sweaty struggle against weeds, all the while clearing more land for next year's crops, then the race to harvest and lay up foodstuffs for man and beast before the first killing frost. The shorter days and harsher weather of December also interrupted outdoor routines in communities that had evolved around timbering for shipbuilding, or mining, or simple manufacturing. Since dreary weather meant lighting the candles early anyway, why not take advantage of the situation and be of good cheer?

Appropriately enough, it was fervent prayers amid flickering candlelight on December 24, 1741, that led to America's first "Christmas city." Moravian settlers, fleeing religious persecution first in their native Bohemia and Czechoslovakia, then in Saxony (Germany), eventually settled on the banks of the Lehigh River in Pennsylvania. A visiting German count joined in their simple candlelight devotions in a log building that also sheltered cattle. Inspired by such humble surroundings, he sang the old German hymn "Not Jerusalem, Lowly Bethlehem," and thus gave the community the name—

Bethlehem—that it bears to this day.

Repetitions of those first Moravian "Love Feasts"—featuring sacred music and carols, a plain yet symbolic meal, and candle-lit vigils—continue to inspire Bethlehem's citizens and visitors today. In other surviving or restored colonial centers and wilderness outposts (often encircled today by noisy, thriving cities), local townspeople and tourists jostle together for a living history lesson and a bit of holiday inspiration.

In Williamsburg, Virginia, just a few miles inland from Jamestown, throngs gather each December for the Grand Illumination. They watch the Militia on parade and hear the Night Watch command tavernkeepers and housewives: "Light your candles!" Evergreen wreaths; intricate centerpieces of magnolia leaves, fruits, and nuts; spruce boughs festooning banisters and mantlepieces; steaming bowls of wassail—all are revealed through the glowing windowpanes. Doors open and vaguely familiar fiddle tunes escape into the night air.

And the Transformation Begins

Amid such vivid reminders, it's easy to imagine how eagerly the colonists awaited the holiday season's gathering of family and friends. Whispers ripple through the cold night air as we assure ourselves, "Yes, yes, *this* is really an American Christmas!"

And yet this was only one of many styles prevalent in the 1770's. As sophisticated and forward-thinking as many colonists were in the political arena, the citizens of Williamsburg and the other cities burgeoning up and down the eastern seaboard and into the country's interior were still relatively isolated from each other, with few opportunities to share holiday traditions. Although the Revolutionary period forced people from different Old World cultures into closer contact with

each other, it wasn't until the 1800's that these various Christmas customs began to mingle freely.

Even then, some ideas were slow to catch on. A few early German immigrants hung simple decorations on Christmas trees in the new land, and an oft-repeated story tells of Washington's troops surprising Hessian mercenaries singing carols around a candle-lit tree. But though it was a staple of Yuletide celebrations in German-American communities in the early nineteenth century, folks elsewhere didn't adopt the idea of decorating trees until an illustration of Queen Victoria's elaborate tree appeared in the fashionable, trend-setting magazine *Godey's Lady's Book*. The first Christmas tree to grace the White House was set up by President Franklin Pierce in 1856.

In the southern plantation states during the period leading up to the Civil War, Christmas festivities for owners and slaves alike lasted as long as the Yule log burned—and there were quite a few clever schemes devised to ensure that its flames lasted at least a week! A popular game first played in the cramped slave cabins soon spread to the airy corridors and rooms of the masters' houses: Whenever two people would meet for the first time on Christmas Day, the first to shout "Christmas Gif' " was entitled to receive an extra treat or hand-made present from the one caught. In the south, African rhythms met Christian stories and soon poignant, joyous spirituals such as "Go Tell It on the Mountain" provided counterpoint for European carols.

Two southern states, Arkansas and Louisiana, were the first to declare December 25 a legal holiday. Alabama followed suit in 1836. But the no-frivolity legacy of the Puritans continued in many northern communities; another 20 years passed before staid Massachusetts got around to such a proclamation.

In a land offering refuge and opportunities to immigrants with sharply varying religious convictions, official agreement on the holiday's true date wasn't easy. Some sects kept the Twelve Days of Christmas, waiting until Epiphany, on January 6, to exchange gifts. In other areas, most notably those with Dutch connections, the holiday got off to an earlier start: Sinterklass roamed about leaving gifts and small treats for children on St. Nicholas' Day, December 6, often with promises of more to follow (but only to *good* little boys and girls) on Christmas morning.

'Twas Christmas Eve, 1822, when Clement C. Moore composed his delightful poem recounting "A Visit from St. Nicholas" to amuse his children. Perhaps borrowing from a contemporary booklet, *The Children's Friend*, which replaced the kindly bishop's horse with a reindeer, and giving the "right jolly old elf" the face and physique of a very real Dutch friend, Moore gave new life to an old legend. The poem rapidly took on a life of its own, being printed, anonymously, in the Troy (New York) *Sentinel* the following Christmas. Over the years it was reprinted in countless papers and magazines, on special single news sheets, sometimes embellished with wood engravings—it became so popular that Moore finally acknowledged authorship in 1837.

Even the uncertainties and horrors of the Civil War couldn't deter Santa from his annual rounds. In 1863, political cartoonist Thomas Nast produced his first illustrations of Moore's poem. For the next 30 years, Nast continued to refine his vision, which became firmly planted in the American consciousness.

Indeed, it wasn't until after the Civil War had settled the issue that we would remain *one* nation that Christmas began to accumulate many of the traditions we hold so dear today. Transportation, communication, and manufacturing all boomed during the late 1800's, making it possible for Americans, no matter where their forefathers came from, to share in a vast popular culture.

After the war, Louis Prang, a German immigrant

who'd been working as a wood engraver and lithographer in Boston since 1850, heard about the new English custom of sending printed Christmas greetings through the mail. Prang's first thought was to get in on the lucrative export market, so in 1874 he printed a selection of cards for shipment to England. They sold so well that the following year he printed even more and kept some for sale in America. The idea caught on and by 1880 he began sponsoring annual competitions (with prizes of up to a thousand dollars) to inspire American artists to create original designs. Soon the mails were clogged with colorful, precisely manufactured cards featuring all manner of imaginative images and verses, and even cards that folded up or out to create three-dimensional scenes.

A different form of Christmas artwork also became prevalent—colorful holiday advertising announcing the latest manufactured goods. Trade cards, handed out in shops or enclosed in packages, publicized upcoming holiday sales and special events, and products ranging from soap to sewing notions, mincemeat to condensed milk. Although homemakers began to associate reliable suppliers and brand names with the ingredients for their holiday concoctions, baking remained essentially a do-it-yourself project.

Advertising and mass-manufacturing, however, had more of an effect in the gift-giving realm. Drums, dolls, toy soldiers, miniature animals and boats, whistles, wooden puzzles—such playthings had brightened the faces and hours of children from the earliest Christmases in America. But in all but the most prosperous families, these gifts weren't bought—some clever family member spent weeks in secret labor lovingly crafting toys and trinkets out of whatever materials were at hand. But as reliable mail service and an ever-expanding network of railroads linked the growing country together, American parents were soon able to choose from a vast array of manufactured goodies. Whether gazing at the profusely illustrated, dramatically worded pages of the Sears and Roebuck catalog or into the jam-packed windows of the toy stores springing up on every Main Street, their children were soon dreaming of—and receiving—wind-up boats and trains, elaborately engineered dollhouses, Noah's Ark and circus animals with moveable joints, colorful boxes and tins of chocolates and hard sugar candies, all made in far-away factories.

These toys appeared under trees laden mostly with hand- and home-made decorations: garlands of popcorn and cranberries, fanciful shapes cut from scraps of colored paper, gilded nuts, cookies, paper horns filled with candies. Recent German immigrants brightened their trees with a few gleaming glass ornaments painstakingly brought over from the Old Country in suitcases and steamer trunks. Then in 1880, F. W. Woolworth offered glass ornaments imported from Germany to the general public—and eager Americans bought every last one within days.

Only one more modification remained to transform the crowded branches of the tree into the glowing symbol of Christmas so familiar today. As breath-taking and inspiring a sight as it may have been, a tree illuminated with candles presented a serious fire hazard. Even with the invention of special clips and tiny dishes to catch drips (and buckets of sand or water nearby in case of accidents), lighting the Christmas tree was a one-night-only treat, closely supervised by adults. It's no wonder that just three years after the invention of the electric light bulb, Americans adapted it to the Christmas tree. New Yorkers gathered in 1882 to watch a unique holiday demonstration: a revolving tree illuminated by 80 flashing lights (red, white, and blue, of course!), and ushered in a new age of trees twinkling day and night throughout the holidays.

'Tis the Season

American Christmas customs stretch back over the centuries, yet the episodes we hold most dear aren't found in the headlines of long-ago newspapers, the fading columns of ledgerbooks, or museums—they're all around us in the holiday rituals we often take for granted. The story of Christmas in America continues to unfold in all its splendor against a backdrop of the myriad activities we enjoy together. Whether we bundle up in overcoats to brave the streets of Manhattan for a glimpse of Santa in Macy's big parade, or begin the countdown to Christmas Day snuggled in our robes and bunny slippers watching it all on TV at home, 'tis the season for family fun—and food!

Peek through the windows of just about any American dining room at Christmas and you're likely to see two treasured native foods, roast turkey and cranberries. But that's just the beginning, for each region has its favorite accompaniments, each ethnic heritage its own special contributions. In the Midwest, where many Scandinavians settled, Christmas dinner wouldn't be complete without *lutefisk*, a pungent fish dish not for the faint of palate. In Italian families *panetone*, a raisin-studded sweet bread, has a place of honor. And in every family, between savory mouthfuls, we chatter on, telling our own private Christmas stories, recalling the time the cat stole the drumstick, the year Jimmy got a pecan shell stuck in his braces, debating whether it was four years ago or five that Aunt Betty put brandy in the sweet potato casserole—and didn't tell anybody!

The feasting and reminiscing aren't confined to dinner, either. In the Southwest, where the Mexican influence is strongest, families returning from Midnight Mass on December 24 enjoy a late-night supper featuring steaming bowls of *posole*, hominy stew flavored with chunks of pork and chilis. In the deep South, Christmas breakfast or brunch is the perfect time to enjoy salty country ham with red-eye gravy, grits dressed up for the holidays with cheese and garlic, and cornbread fresh from the oven.

And from Freeport to Fresno, from Great Falls to Greater Miami, holiday cookery means sweets. Fruit-cakes, pies, coconut cupcakes, cookies, candies, even hot and cold beverages prove that sugar is *the* one unifying theme in American kitchens. At Thanksgiving we may be satisfied with pumpkin and pecan pies, but come Christmas we want to have it *all*. German *springerles*, Swiss almond tea wafers, gingerbread cookies, chocolate stars, English plum pudding, Kentucky Bourbon balls, pecan pralines, eggnog—glossy magazines and even whole cookbooks devoted to the subject entice us to sample new combinations every December.

An old saying claims that the proof of the pudding is in the eating, but during December the pleasure often begins in the kitchen. In the early twilight, a small boy drags a chair across the linoleum and climbs up to stand at his mother's elbow. Flour and nutmeg, eggs and sugar are all arrayed on the countertop in readiness. The woman scans the delicate handwriting on the smudged and slightly tattered recipe and sees not just a listing of ingredients, but a long-ago kitchen. She places the little boy's hand over hers and says, "Help me sift this flour and I'll tell you about your great-grandmother. She taught me how to make these cookies a long, long time ago. She wore a big red apron, just about the color of your sweater—and it had flour all over it, too, just like you do. . ." and we discover a way to make time stand still.

Of course, children perceive things a bit differently—the toddler accompanying her older sisters and brothers for *Las Posadas* (the candle-lit procession of families and friends recreating Mary and Joseph's search for room

at an inn over the nine evenings from December 16 through Christmas Eve) doesn't know she's following a centuries-old Southwestern American tradition—she just knows that at the end, this year she'll get a chance to break the *piñata*. And maybe, just maybe, she'll capture the biggest piece of candy in the mad scramble that follows.

Wide-eyed youngsters in Sun Valley, Idaho, haven't a clue who first thought of organizing a parade of torch-carrying skiers. They just "ooh" and "aah" along with the grown-ups as the snow-covered slopes are gradually transformed into a flickering, golden wonderland—and wish fervently for Santa to bring them skis this year. Far away, in a little harbor in Florida, other children gaze in awe at twinkling masts of sailboats, outlined with strings of tiny electric lights, bobbing and swaying with the tide—and quietly eavesdrop in astonishment as Mom and Dad hold hands and whisper to each other about the first Christmas they spent together.

In a suburb of Nashville, other children wiggle and squirm next to Grandpa in the ample backseat of a much-used station wagon for the customary Saturday-before-Christmas tour of a neighborhood famed for its extravagant display of decorations. Yards of rooftops gleam with every possible permutation on Santa, reindeer, snowmen, elves, angels, carolers, bigger-than-life candy canes—until Grandpa exclaims (exactly as he did last year and the year before that), "We never had anything like this when *I* was your age!"

In a crowded lobby in Louisville, boys in bow ties and girls in ruffles submit to last-minute inspections by their elders as the houselights blink to signal the beginning of yet another performance of Dickens' *A Christmas Carol*. In Dallas and Denver and dozens of other cities throughout America, grown-ups prepare to introduce the younger generation to the splendor of Bach's *Christmas Oratorio* and the magic of *The*

Nutcracker. Settled at last in their seats, Aunt Martha momentarily forgets that she's watched and listened to this classic a dozen times before, and experiences it anew as she secretly observes her nephews and nieces.

From Boston to Bakersfield, on the latest big-screen TVs and third-hand portable sets, with plates of warm cookies close at hand, young and old alike get a bit misty-eyed at each twist of the plot in *It's a Wonderful Life, Miracle on 34th Street, Amahl and the Night Visitors,* even *The Grinch Who Stole Christmas.* In households with children of a certain age, it just isn't Christmas until everyone joins in to recite favorite lines along with the characters on the screen.

And then there's the tradition of shopping—better start with the tree. Should it be tall, with lots of space between the limbs to show off the ornaments, or short and full? Already cut and hanging at the Boy Scouts' corner lot? Or a still living tree, its burlap root ball holding the promise of spring? Or shall we all pile into the car for a drive way out in the country to cut our own? Or maybe a tree that's not a tree at all, but a magical construction of chrome and plastic? And don't forget some new ornaments and more tinsel and say, wouldn't another string of lights be nice?

The exhortations to buy, buy, buy start as early as September with those late night TV ads insisting, "Order *now* for delivery by Christmas!" By October, the postman's staggering under the weight of all those catalogs to deliver. November comes and you can tell how many shopping days remain simply by the weight of the Sunday newspaper, as every store for miles around proclaims, "Doors Open at 8:00 A.M.!" "Open 'til Midnight!" "Convenient Lay-A-Way Terms!" We make our lists and check them twice, comparing prices and sizes, searching for something besides handkerchiefs for dear old Uncle John. Mom and Dad take turns with the kids, helping each to select a gift for the other parent,

and making sure it stays a secret until Christmas. 'Tis the season for whispers and tiptoeing down to the basement for more wrapping paper, and yes, even hand-made gifts.

The Everlasting Light

And though the glitter and glitz threatens at times to overwhelm, there are still plenty of Americans who usher in the season with an age-old custom: lighting the candles of the Advent Wreath, one for each of the four Sundays preceding Christmas. We read from the Bible and pray, in the privacy of our own homes, then gather in tiny chapels and huge cathedrals to contemplate the true purpose of our celebrations.

We pause during the seemingly endless rounds of shopping and baking and decorating to reflect on the story that begins "And it came to pass in those days. . ." and find ourselves drawn to a very different living history lesson. For this one takes place on a thousand churchyard lawns, where ordinary folks stand in a Living Manger Scene. Friends and neighbors, even strangers, gather in the darkness to watch, and in the cool night air each hears, deep in his or her own private reverie, a voice singing, "O little town of Bethlehem, how still we see thee lie. . . ."

The words express an Episcopal minister's thoughts after an arduous journey to Bethlehem, and were intended to instruct the children in his Philadelphia Sunday School. Yet they were almost lost to us, for the church organist struggled for a week to set the verses to music, then fell into bed exhausted the night before the song was supposed to be played. He closed his eyes without so much as the first note ready. But during the night, he awoke suddenly from his sleep and jotted down the entire melody—it was, he said later, "a gift from Heaven."

Through the mysterious power of music, Christmas speaks to our hearts, perhaps most delightfully in the ceremony of the Living Christmas Tree. Ranks of choir members, carefully wedged in place amid a pyramid of greenery, fill the sanctuary with the songs of Christmas, inviting the congregation to sing along. For though we enjoy being spectators, we want to participate, to somehow become *part* of the action. And Christmas carols provide the perfect means to express the deep emotions of the season—no special clothes or even any musical training is needed to join in the singing. We learn carols simply by listening, over and over again, until we know the words and tunes "by heart," their lilting melodies and simple refrains inspiring us anew each December. At church and at home, gathered on a neighbor's doorstep, or even out shopping, we lift our voices in hope.

We sing "Jingle Bells" and "Silver Bells" and "I Heard the Bells on Christmas Day" (all by American composers)—and cheerfully answer the insistent clanging of Salvation Army handbells with the clink of pocket change filling up those symbolic black kettles. But in the spirit of the Old World carol "Good King Wenceslas," American Christmas charity isn't just in the form of money—we like to give by doing. Volunteer firemen give even more of their time to gather Toys for Tots, then distribute them to needy children. Service clubs of all sorts spring into action to provide food and clothing, even shelter, for the less fortunate. Still other groups and big-hearted individuals find ways to brighten the hours of prisoners, hospital patients, and nursing home residents who might otherwise be forgotten by singing carols, decorating, or playing Santa. In peace or in war, the USO and the Red Cross provide entertainment and a link with home for service men and women stationed far from family and friends.

Home for the Holidays

Though we each carry a vision of what the Nativity must have been like, reinforced by the images on thousands of Christmas cards, living manger scenes on church lawns, and the poetic lines of carols and hymns, come December our thoughts turn again and again to the places, events, and people of our own lives. We have a deep and fierce longing to spend Christmas with our families. For when you get right down to it, the very best Christmas stories are the little dramas played out within each and every American family.

We move here from different lands, we move around from city to city, from the homes of our childhood to apartments to houses and back to apartments, carrying with us little vignettes of Christmases past. And with each year we add to the kaleidoscope of images, adding more chapters to the story of Christmas in America.

So after you've told the children about the Baby Jesus and Santa Claus and reindeer and the Star of Bethlehem, let your mind's eye wander through those cherished memories. Let workaday worries and cares fade away and concentrate on bringing the colors and textures of your holiday reverie into sharper focus. Holding that vision clearly in mind and the children on your lap, tell them a story of Christmas as you've experienced it. Tell them of noisy celebrations and quiet moments by the fireside, of kisses under the mistletoe and candy canes in stockings, of grandparents and aunts and uncles and cousins and the little old lady next door. Share your vision in a story—a Christmas story that's sure to be an American original.

May you have the gladness of Christmas
Which is hope;
The spirit of Christmas
Which is peace;
The heart of Christmas
Which is love.

Ada V. Hendricks

Homeward bound: Checking the rope looped
round the saddlehorn just one more time,
and murmuring soft words of encouragement
to their horse, a Colorado father and child
enjoy a traditional holiday task—finding the
"perfect" Christmas tree.

With Mom and Dad to worry about
such details as keeping a firm grip on
the Christmas tree and guiding the sled
over the snow-laden slopes of Vail,
Colorado, the kids are free to laugh and
sing all the way home.

When the snow's this deep in
Vermont, there's only one thing to
do—let the nacksaw dangle from
your elbow, hoist the tree up on your
shoulders, whistle for the dog, and
keep repeating, "Christmas comes
but once a year."

In Colorado's high mountain country, a savvy cowboy takes the right gear along on a Christmas tree "round-up": gleaming lantern, stout rope, wide-brimmed hat—and snowshoes!

Warmed up after a morning of farm chores, this Vermont couple takes their tractor on the road for a bit of holiday tree shopping.

19

Preceding page: December sun gives a pearly
luster to new-fallen snow in Walton, New York.
Above: Frost particles form elegant patterns on
a windowpane in Lyons Falls, New York.

In the heart of midtown Manhattan, larger-than-life-size buglers and stylized angels herald the Yuletide season at Rockefeller Center. Long before the buildings were completed, construction crews inaugurated a custom that still lives on—they erected the first Christmas tree on the site in 1931.

Young trumpeters make a joyful noise at Mission San Jose
in Texas.

Salvation Army musicians, such as this tuba player in
Chicago, turn city streets into outdoor concert halls—and
inspire us to give generously so that all may share in
the season's joy.

In Aspen, Colorado, carolers don winter clothing from a bygone era for their Yuletide serenades.

Even His Honor the Mayor finds time to sing along with the carolers at Dollywood in Pigeon Forge, Tennessee.

"Deck the halls with boughs of holly, Fa-la-la-la. . . ." Against a backdrop of
evergreen wreaths and graceful garlands, life-size lawn decorations in
Lenox, Massachusetts, form a favorite tableau.

Thousands of carolers mass together in New
Orleans' Jackson Square for an evening of Christmas
songs and hymns.

Flickering candlelight casts a cheery
glow on Louisiana carolers...

...while in Santa Fe, New Mexico,
a traditional bonfire warms
Christmas Eve singers.

A fife and drum corps in Colonial
Williamsburg, Virginia, recreates the sights and
sounds of a Revolutionary Christmas.

*J*oy to the World! The Saviour reigns;
Let men their songs employ;
While fields and floods, rocks, hills, and plains
Repeat the sounding joy,
Repeat the sounding joy,
Repeat, Repeat the sounding joy.

Isaac Watts

Living Christmas trees—choirs carefully
arranged in towering pyramids—have become a
favorite Yuletide tradition throughout America.
Here mittened tenors, basses, altos, and sopranos
endure chilly Atlantic breezes to harmonize at
New York City's South Street Seaport.

December sunlight on snow-clad pines on Tennessee's great Smoky Mountains surpasses any greeting card artist's invention.

Mid-winter snow adds an extra aura of mystery to Yellowstone National Park's famed geysers (left) and highlights the majestic contours of California's Yosemite Valley (overleaf).

A team of willing draft horses gives holiday skiers
an unusual "lift" at Sugarloaf Ski Resort in
western Maine.

The merry jingle of harness bells along a back road
near Salt Lake City, Utah, proclaims,
"Company's coming!"

*T*here are sounds in the sky when the year grows old,
    And the winds of the winter blow—
When nights and the moon are clear and cold,
    And the stars shine on the snow.
Or wild is the blast and the bitter sleet
    That beats on the window-pane;
But blest on the frosty hills the feet
    Of the Christmas time again!

Anonymous

In Vermont, a one-horse open sleigh still sets
the pace in December.

On the wind-swept shores of Lake Michigan, a Chicago coach driver tends to last-minute details as the horses wait patiently to begin their holiday rounds.

A full moon, incandescent bulbs by the millions, and the
famous skyline of San Francisco, California, combine
for an eye-dazzling panorama.

At San Francisco's Embarcadero
Center, graceful curves invite
closer inspection, while the
lights on the office buildings,
arranged with geometric
precision, draw the eye
skyward.

Christmas lights outline the Spanish-style buildings
at the Country Club Plaza in Kansas City,
Missouri.

Masses of shimmering lights create a visual symphony under
the dark December sky in Baton Rouge, Louisiana...

. . . with a decidedly Southern flair!

Christmas in America's capital: The timeless
message on the White House banner reminds us of
the true meaning of the season.

Whether it's the star-spangled, multi-colored splendor of the immense National Christmas Tree . . .

. . . or the understated elegance of a tree clad entirely in tiny white lights, Yuletide traditions and decorations add a festive flair to our most treasured landmarks in Washington, D.C.

47

In this reindeer's-eye view of Chicago, even the headlights and taillights of vehicles moving along Michigan Avenue contribute to the holiday glow.

At street level, friends linger hand in hand for another look at leafless trees dressed in holiday finery.

The Space Needle, festooned with gleaming lights, crowns Seattle,
Washington's skyline like a giant's plaything.

More than meets the eye: What first appears to be
a castle reflected in a moat is actually the Mormon
Temple in Kensington, Maryland . . .

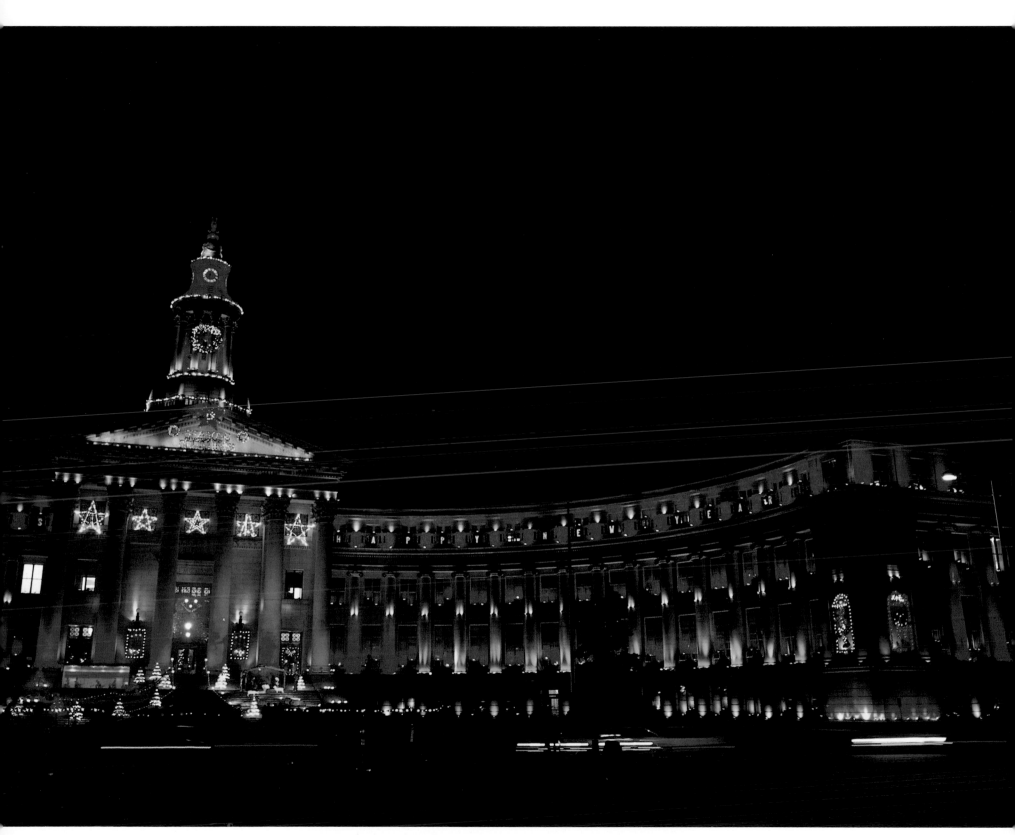

. . . and this Chinese pagoda is really Denver, Colorado's City and County
Building "painted" with the glow of a thousand colored spotlights.

From a Cleveland shopping mall with beribboned lamp-posts and balconies trimmed all in miniature white bulbs, to a towering Minneapolis skyscraper crowned with a radiant star . . .

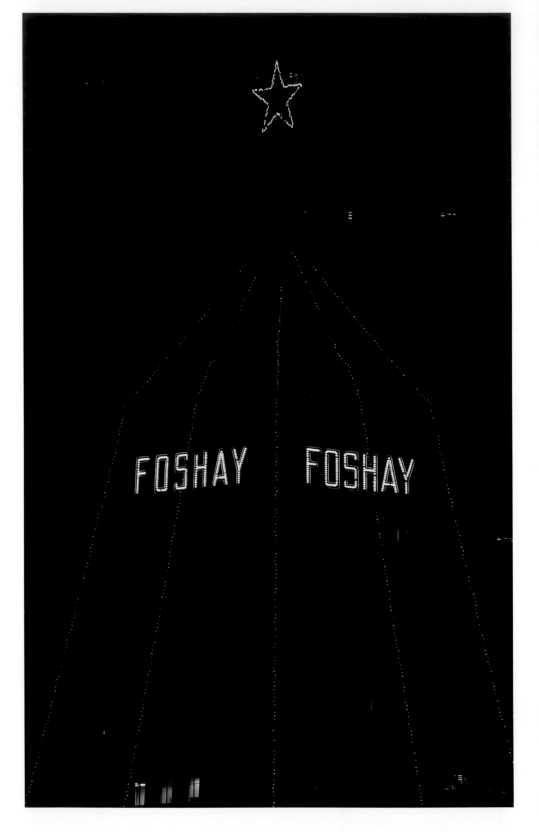

*S*ilent night, holy night,
All is calm, all is bright.

Joseph Mohr

. . . to glittering trees in a palatial Salt Lake
City churchyard garden, Christmas in
America is a festival of light.

Though the familiar beacon of Maine's Nubble Lighthouse
warns mariners to beware of danger, in December
twinkling strings of multi-colored Christmas lights send a
message of good cheer.

Abundant loops and swirls of lights transform San
Antonio, Texas' Riverwalk into a fairytale
kingdom.

I *heard a bird sing*
  In the dark of December
A magical thing
  And sweet to remember.

"We are nearer to Spring
  Than we were in September,"
I heard a bird sing
  In the dark of December.

Oliver Herford

In the foothills of the Cascade Mountains
along Oregon's Willamette Valley, row after
row of future Christmas trees wait under a
blanket of snow.

Left: Eager youngsters besiege Father Christmas for peppermint candy canes at the annual Christmas Festival in Georgetown, Colorado. *Above:* It's beginning to look a lot like Christmas in Naples, Florida, when bicycle baskets overflow with brightly colored packages.

Walking oh-so-carefully in a winter wonderland,
a little girl in Jefferson, Maine, struggles to keep a
firm grip on her present—and her feet firmly
on the icy path!

Will the *real* Santa please step forward? At the Crystal Palace Mall in Santa Ana, California, that "right jolly old elf" resembles a grizzled miner from the Gold Rush days...

...while a blue-jeans clad Cajun seems to have been the inspiration for this diminutive Santa hitching a ride on a gaping alligator at Acadian Village in Lafayette, Louisiana.

A totem-like Santa crafted by
chainsaw carver Milo Marshall
stands watch in Stowe, Vermont . . .

. . . while a roadside colossus
welcomes shoppers at Bronner's
Christmas Emporium in
Frankenmuth, Michigan.

An ever-vigilant pair of toy soldiers stands guard over
Cartier's jewelry store on New York City's Fifth Avenue.
Opposite: In Claremont, New Hampshire, a more playful duo
seems ready for a romp in a sparkling winter park.

Santa paddling a canoe? Well, as the old saying goes "you gotta know the territory"—and Santa's stretches from sea to shining sea and beyond!

Yes Virginia, there is
a Santa Claus. He exists
as certainly as love and
generosity and devotion
exist, and you know that
they abound and give to
your life its highest beauty
and joy.

Francis P. Church

Here he takes advantage of binoculars to check
out the neighborhood in New York City . . .

. . . then dons skier's goggles for a
downhill run in Steamboat,
Colorado . . .

. . . which he trades for snorkeling
gear at Lake Worth, Florida . . .

66

. . . and then he hitches a ride in an outrigger to arrive at the
Kihala Hilton in Hawaii.

Windsurfing's a bit tricky with that
ample belly, but no matter how
Santa travels...

...it's getting there that counts!

In San Antonio, a kindly serape- and sombrero-clad Santa is the center of attention.

On New York City's Fifth Avenue at Rockefeller Center, a weary sidewalk Santa takes advantage of a lull in the action for a moment of quiet reflection.

*C*hristmas won't
be Christmas without
any presents.

Louisa May Alcott

Grown-ups say the road to a friend's house is
never long—and this little girl pulling a sled
full of gaily wrapped Christmas presents over
a snowy path in Jefferson, Maine, seems
determined to prove it.

From the suburbs of Virginia . . .

. . . to the streets of Lake Tahoe, California, even automobiles
occasionally serve as the inspiration for holiday decorations.

An eye-dazzling display of holiday symbols stretches from the top of the roof to the edge of the sidewalk in front of a private residence in Queens, New York. There's even room for a tribute to the pope.

Let there be light: Even in this
electrified, electronic age, candles
still work their magic. Brightly
colored Japanese paper lanterns cast
a warm glow on snow-covered
shrubbery along a stairway in
Fairbanks, Alaska . . .

. . . while golden *luminarias* line
a sidewalk in Albany, California.

In Santa Fe, New Mexico, hundreds of *farolitos* outline the adobe balconies
and roof ledges of the Inn of the Alameda.

Winter lasts a long time in Minnesota, so why not
indulge?

In Massachusetts, a gleaming
Christmas tree in a dinghy adds an
air of enchantment and mystery to
Nantucket's frozen shores.

Early December twilight reveals
a sailor's handiwork in Savannah,
Georgia.

Two traditions meet: In Santa Fe, Pueblo Indian pottery figures provide the perfect accent on a pine cone wreath (above), while a fresh dusting of snow adds a cooling Yuletide touch to *ristras* of red chilis (right).

In Orange County, California, the tree's real but the snow is—er, well—let's just keep it a secret, OK?

That powdery white stuff blanketing the ground under this St. Petersburg, Florida, tree isn't snow—but alabaster sand is about as close to a ''white'' Christmas as you can expect this far south!

As if encrusted with specks of molten lava, extravagantly
decorated trees and shrubs in Lantana, Florida, evoke ''oohs''
and ''aahs'' from locals and tourists alike.

Lagniappe—that's the word folks in Louisiana use to describe
an unexpected extra gift. In the early evening stillness before
the merrymaking begins, reflections on the bayou add just
such a special ambiance to the holiday decor at Acadian
Village in Lafayette.

The elegant simplicity of bare tree limbs glistening with
strings of white lights enhances the beauty of RiverPlace in
the heart of Portland, Oregon. *Opposite:* Like a starlet's
rhinestones, shimmering swags and cascades of lights
adorn the Beverly Wilshire Hotel in Los Angeles.

Simple pleasures: An ephemeral coating of frost crystals gives the green leaves and red berries of a common shrub in Santa Rosa, California (left), an uncommon grandeur, while the perfect proportions of a single red bow add a dramatic accent to a New York City holiday wreath (above).

Though the path and steps are covered with snow, luxuriant garlands, a plump wreath, and crimson bows send a cheery invitation to all in Deerfield, Massachusetts.

Even in balmy Savannah, Georgia, the front door of the Eliza Thompson House sports evergreen swags and red ribbons.

In the historic district of Odessa,
Delaware, near Winterthur Museum
and Garden, clusters of scarlet holly
berries amid a handful of greenery
brighten a gate hinge . . .

. . . while a wreath featuring
wooden horses and shiny sleighbells
suggests Christmases long past in
the Georgetown section of
Washington, D.C.

A generous portion of snow, though a bit
inconvenient for shoppers, enhances the
Christmas decor of an old-fashioned emporium in
Newcastle, Maine.

Canine statues sporting wreaths and red bows add
a whimsical touch to the sunlight-dappled
decorations on the front porch of a historic home
in Houston, Texas.

Near Cambridge, Wisconsin, a silo silhouetted
against dusk's amber sheen reveals a farmer's faith.

Precise rows of brilliant white lights boldly outline
a farm near St. George, Delaware.

After an afternoon of sledding, Minnesota youngsters trudge back home
with one thought—will there be warm cookies waiting?

No doubt the Vermont Country Store in Weston holds a fabulous array of Christmas gifts, but fresh snow falling holds more charm for this young skier headed for the slopes.

Hey, wait for me! Oh, well, runaway sleds are just part of the fun in Harrington Park, New Jersey—and on slippery hills everywhere!

From gilded statues and stunning
displays of lights . . .

. . . to the ice-skating rink and scores
of shops, New York City's Rockefeller
Center offers a variety of Christmas
delights that are sure to please.

Radio City Music Hall's famous Rockettes prepare to execute one of their
trademark precision drills during the Parade of the Wooden Soldiers in the
annual Christmas Spectacular in New York City.

Left: Tucked away on a southern back road in Lafayette, Louisiana, flowers and lovingly crafted, hand-made decorations adorn a shrine to the Blessed Virgin and a simple manger scene in front of a time-worn home. *Above:* Taking a closer look at a life-size *nacimiento,* a young Pasadena, California, couple and their children discover anew the wonders of the original Christmas story.

The outdoor Nativity scene at the public library in
Bethlehem, Pennsylvania, even includes the
Wise Men's camels.

Though an abundant display of twinkling lights and other Christmas symbols threaten to overwhelm this Fairbanks, Alaska, home, the manger scene's radiant figures remind passersby of the cause for our celebrations. *Opposite:* The figure of an awe-struck shepherd graces the exquisitely decorated gardens of the Mormon Temple in Oakland, California.

*A*nd it came to pass, as
the angels were gone away from
them into heaven, the shepherds
said one to another, Let us now
go even unto Bethlehem, and
see this thing which is come to
pass, which the Lord hath
made known unto us.

The Gospel According to Luke

In this Salt Lake City Nativity scene, even
the sheep have followed the Star to
Bethlehem. An old folk tradition holds that
each year, as the hour of Jesus' birth
approaches, animals enjoy the gift
of human speech.

All eyes gaze with rapt attention upon the
newborn baby Jesus in this Frankenmuth,
Michigan, Nativity scene.

From tiny crossroads settlements to multi-million-soul metropolises, more than 340,000 churches play a vital role in American lives. In Cambridge, Ohio, neighbors and friends gather for a candlelight Christmas service.

The choir of Trinity Baptist Church in San Antonio, leads the congregation for an evening of carols, anthems, and hymns.

Time-lapse photography captures part of the
mysterious power of candlelight uniting worshipers
at the First Baptist Church in New London,
New Hampshire.

In San Antonio, two angels await
their cue to join *Las Posadas,* the
annual reenactment of Mary and
Joseph's long search for an inn.

Snowflakes come gently to rest
on the ornate carvings and simple
greenery high atop stately Trinity
Church in Boston, Massachusetts.

Preceding pages: Do snowmen know how to sing? If so, you can bet this jaunty quartet in Waterbury, Vermont, knows all the jolliest tunes. *Left:* A strand of chili pepper lights, the Lone Star flag, and a map leave no doubt this tree's in Texas—and when Santa sees that miniature saddle, do you think he'll get the hint? *Above:* In Baraboo, Wisconsin, Santa Claus rests on a porch swing while waiting to make sure the children are *really* ''nestled all snug in their beds.''

This pleasingly plump tree, laden with dozens of candy canes, snowflakes, the traditional assortment of rotund ornaments, and yards of red and gold garland provides a charming focal point in a New York City living room.

All manner of hand-crafted decorations
vie for attention in this Atlanta,
Georgia, parlor, but the hand-carved
figurines jostled together on the mantel
dominate the scene.

*C*ome, sing a hale Heigh-ho
For the Christmas long ago!—
When the old log cabin homed us
From the night of blinding snow.

Where the rarest joy held reign,
And the chimney roared amain,
With the firelight like a beacon
Through the frosty windowpane.

James Whitcomb Riley

Whether it's quilting with a patriotic motif . . .

. . . or petit point based on
European designs . . .

. . . or sampler-style cross-
stitching, nimble fingers and
loving hearts continue to create
one-of-a-kind Christmas heirlooms
in Salisbury, Massachusetts.

Forgotten in boxes stashed deep
in a New York City basement for
eleven months of the year, tiny
treasures once again brighten spirits
come December.

In Williamsburg, Virginia, colorful
scraps from the sewing basket, corn
husks, even wood shavings take on a
new life as colonial-style Christmas
ornaments.

On a Victorian-style tree in Los Angeles, California, a frosted glass angel strums a lute . . .

. . . for a porcelain ballerina.

Two stout Virginians take time out from the usual
workday routines to perform a pleasant holiday
chore—bringing the Yule log to Williamsburg Inn.

Hope springs eternal on Christmas
Eve—surely, from somewhere deep
in his sack, Old Saint Nick will draw
forth a nice chewy bone.

Although intent on getting a
glimpse of Santa Claus, this
Pasadena, California, brother and
sister seem to have fallen asleep
during their vigil.

*A*t Christmas play and make good cheer
For Christmas comes but once a year.

Thomas Tusser

**In Ossining, New York, the wait is over—
at last!**

Three generations of a Richmond, Virginia, family
share in the fun.

In Bozeman, Montana, a little girl proves once again that it's
not the size of the gift that matters, but the spirit in which
it's offered—and in which it's received!

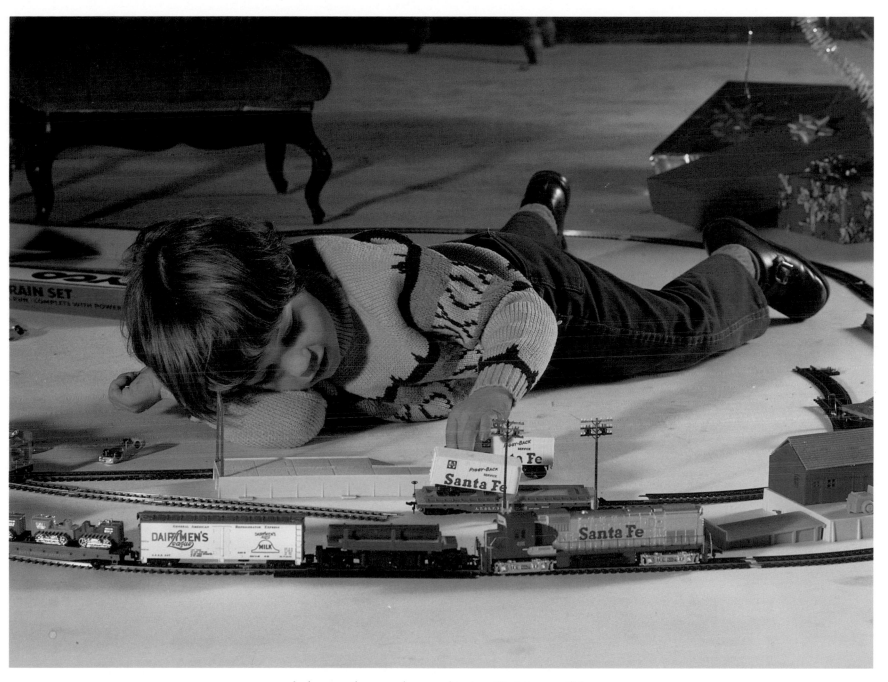

As long as there are boys and trains, Christmas will be
a time of enchantment.

At New Mexico's San Ildefonso Pueblo, Christmas Day
celebrations now include the Annual Buffalo Dance.
Though the Native American drummers wear modern
clothing, the rhythms go back to the time of the
Ancient Ones . . .

. . . and the designs of the dancers' traditional
costumes and adornments have been handed
down reverently through countless generations.

'*T*was Christmas broached the mightiest a
'*Twas Christmas told the merriest tale;*
A Christmas gambol oft could cheer
A poor man's heart through half the year.

Sir Walter Sco

At New York City's Federal Hall, a light
dusting of snow adds an ethereal beauty to a
massive statue, its arm outstretched as if to
reach down to touch the glimmering
Christmas tree far below.

In a Plymouth, Massachusetts, colonial kitchen still redolent with the aromas of the day's cooking, the table's set with a Christmas feast. *Above:* The Christmas that began our nation: In 1776, while British and Hessian troops lingered long over their holiday meals and indulged in Christmas Day games and sport, General George Washington took advantage of their failure to post a guard and managed to cross the Delaware River undiscovered to rout them from their encampment. That daring raid inspired American soldiers throughout the long Revolutionary War—and is proudly reenacted each Christmas in Bucks County, Pennsylvania.

INDEX OF PHOTOGRAPHY

All photographs courtesy of The Image Bank, except where indicated*.